THE NATIONAL TRUST

Investigating

THE CIVIL WAR

By Alison Honey
Illustrated by Peter Stevenson

Contents

D1446136

THE STORY OF THE WAR

CHARLES I DISMISSING PARLIAMENT

The background

When Charles became King in 1625, Puritan members of Parliament outnumbered the Anglicans and Catholics in the House of Commons. Charles I, however, seemed to favour Catholics and made William Laud, a fierce opponent of the Puritans, Archbishop of Canterbury. The Puritans were also suspicious of Charles because he had a Catholic wife, Henrietta Maria, and was surrounded by Catholics at Court.

In 1629 Charles became fed up with Parliament and dismissed all its members. For eleven years he tried to rule the country without them. After trying to force the Scots to use the Church of England prayerbook Charles went to war with Scotland.

Charles had boxed himself in a corner as he needed Parliament to vote money to finance his wars against the Scots and the Irish. In 1640 he recalled Parliament but they refused to impose taxes and Charles dismissed them after only three weeks. After another defeat at the hands of the Scots, he again recalled Parliament who took the upper hand and demanded the imprisonment and execution of his chief minister, the Earl of Strafford, and the unpopular, Archbishop Laud. Strafford was executed and Laud was imprisoned in the Tower of London for five years before being executed in 1645.

In an effort to restore his command of the situation, Charles decided to arrest the five main Parliamentarian ring leaders. This was the final straw for the Parliamentarians – rebellion broke out on the streets of London, and civil war was just round the corner.

WAR!

1642
Charles I left London for York. After the Earl of Essex had raised a Parliamentary army in the Midlands, the King set up his standard in Nottingham in August. In October the Royalists set out for London. The battle of Edgehill in Warwickshire was a draw, with both sides claiming they'd won. The Royalists advanced on London but were turned back at Turnham Green in Essex. Charles made Oxford his base for the rest of the war.

1643
The Royalists concentrated on securing the West. They won a resounding victory at Roundway Down in Wiltshire and captured Bristol but were held up by the siege of Gloucester.

1644
The tide began to turn against the Royalists. In January the Scottish army came to the support of Parliament. In July the King's nephew, Prince Rupert, was defeated at Marston Moor near York and the Royalists lost the North.

1645

In England several Parliamentary forces were linked to form the efficient New Model Army commanded by Sir Thomas Fairfax. In June at the battle of Naseby in Northamptonshire the Parliamentarians won a decisive victory. The following month the last Royalist army, commanded by George Goring, was defeated at Langport in Somerset.

1646–1648

In May 1646 Charles took refuge with the Scots. He failed to come to terms with them and in January 1647 they surrendered him to Parliament. The following year scattered Royalist risings broke out but were all unsuccessful. Meanwhile the New Model Army seized Charles and occupied London. Charles escaped to the Isle of Wight, gave himself up to the Parliamentarian governor and was held prisoner at Carisbrooke Castle.

1649

Charles I was tried, found guilty and executed.

1650

Charles II, who had been crowned King in Scotland after his father's execution, formed an alliance with the Scots who were then defeated by Cromwell at the battle of Dunbar in Scotland.

1651

Charles II led a Scottish army into England reaching Worcester before being defeated by the Parliamentarian army.

1653

Cromwell was appointed Lord Protector. Dissatisfied with the rule of Parliament, he divided England into districts each controlled by a major-general. Military rule was ruthless and effective but unpopular and the system only lasted two years.

1658

Cromwell died and was succeeded as Lord Protector by his son, Richard.

1659

Richard Cromwell resigned and the Council of the Army recalled the Long Parliament. George Monck, commanding the army in Scotland, returned to London and under his influence a new Parliament was elected which voted for the return of Charles II.

1660

On 29th May, to great rejoicing, Charles II re-entered London as King.

THE MAIN CHARACTERS

Royalists

King Charles I
1600–49

Charles was a deeply religious man. He believed that he had been chosen by God to rule the country and that anyone who questioned him was questioning God's will. He was horrified by Parliament's opposition to his authority and was prepared to die rather than give in to their demands.

Rupert, Prince Palatine of the Rhine
1619–82

Rupert was Charles's nephew. Known as the 'Mad Cavalier', he was a brilliant military commander but was proud and headstrong and many of the other Royalist commanders disliked him. He was responsible for many brave but undisciplined cavalry charges and fought at the battles of Edgehill, Marston Moor and Naseby. He was made Commander-in-Chief of the Royalist forces at the age of twenty-five but Charles never really forgave him for surrendering at the siege of Bristol.

George Goring, Earl of Norwich
1608–57

Goring was a strange man – a skilled soldier who had a cruel streak. His troops were known for their ill-discipline and ran riot through the countryside of the west of England. He was also very fond of the bottle and his drunkenness led to unpopularity with Charles. He was in command of the Royalist army defeated at Langport.

Charles II
1630–85

Charles was only a young boy when the Civil War broke out but, as the King's eldest son, was still an important figurehead, and was present at the battle of Edgehill. In 1644 when the Royalists' fortunes were turning, he was sent abroad for safety and spent time in the Scilly Isles, Jersey and France. After the execution of his father he led an unsuccessful attack against the Roundheads which was smashed at the battle of Worcester in 1651. He escaped to the Continent again, and spent a lot of time in Holland. Nine years later he returned to London as King.

Parliamentary Commanders
Oliver Cromwell
1599–1658

Cromwell quickly made his mark as a brilliant military commander with highly disciplined troops. A blunt, middle-aged countryman he had no time for airs and graces and declared that he 'would rather have a plain, russet-coated captain that knows what he fights for and loves what he knows, than that which you call a gentleman and is nothing else'. He believed that he had been chosen by God to free England of Charles's reign. He was appointed Lord Protector of England and Head of the Commonwealth after the execution of Charles I.

Robert Devereux, Earl of Essex
1591–1646

The Earl of Essex was a brave and trustworthy man, though not a brilliant tactician. He commanded the main Parliamentary army from 1642 to 1644. He started the war pessimistically by taking his coffin and shroud around the country with him! He was responsible for relieving the siege of Gloucester in 1643.

Sir Thomas Fairfax
1612–71

Known as 'Black Tom', Sir Thomas Fairfax was an extremely successful military commander. In 1644 he was made commander of the New Model Army, the efficient and disciplined force which was largely responsible for the defeat of the Royalists. He was young, gentle and polite and had a loyal following among his native Yorkshiremen. His wife was a strict Puritan, but also a Royalist, and Fairfax refused to sign the death warrant of King Charles I.

OLIVER CROMWELL

HENRY IRETON

Henry Ireton
1611–51

Ireton was a lawyer by trade, not a soldier. He led a troop of cavalry at the battle of Naseby but was captured by the Royalists. He was Cromwell's son-in-law and one of the fifty-nine men who signed Charles I's death warrant. He was sent to Ireland in 1649 by Cromwell to deal with rebellion. His body was dug up at the Restoration, beheaded, and reburied at Tyburn.

SIR THOMAS FAIRFAX

AND THE NEW MODEL ARMY

WARFARE, WEAPONS AND DRESS

Warfare during the Civil War was often a slow business. A cannon could only fire one ball every three minutes. Count to 180, and you'll see that's not very fast.

Quick fire?

Even guns and muskets were not much quicker. A well-trained soldier might be able to fire his matchlock off once a minute but in order to do any effective damage, and hit his target, the soldier could not be more than fifty metres away. Another problem with these guns was that they had to be fired by using a lighted match or taper and were more or less useless in bad weather. The musket was probably most effective when it was used against people in hand-to-hand fighting.

Charge!

A cavalryman usually carried a pair of pistols, but was much more likely to use his sword in hand-to-hand combat. The cavalry charge, when the closely packed cavalry would attack at the gallop, was one of the most effective ways of fighting.

The Main Battles of the Civil War

Dunbar 1650

Marston Moor 1644

Naseby 1645

Worcester 1651

Edgehill 1642

Newbury 1643 & 1644

Roundway Down 1643

Langport 1645

The soldiers

Cavalry Officer

Cuirassier

Royalist Sergeant

Roundhead Pikeman

Musketeer

7

Troops of hedgehogs

Pikemen moved in a formation called a hedgehog, closely packed together with their pikes pointing up as the 'spines' of the hedgehog. Musketeers, who fought with no armour, would retreat under the hedgehog when they came under heavy musket or cannon fire from the enemy.

Man the hoes!

When the war began, there weren't enough weapons to equip all the volunteers, and many ended up fighting with pitchforks and farm tools.

Armour

Some soldiers on horseback wore full armour which would have been extremely uncomfortable and awkward, especially if the soldier was unlucky enough to fall off his horse. It would have been practically impossible for him to remount without help.

Fact file

One hundred thousand Englishmen were killed in action in the Civil War out of a population of five million. Many more died from wounds, sickness and hunger.

Mistaken identity

It was often difficult identifying soldiers on the battlefield, as troops from the Royalist and Parliamentarian sides would sometimes wear similar clothes and there was no established uniform. There are records of at least two Royalist officers being captured when they mistook an enemy regiment for their own.

Civil War search

Can you find eleven names of battles and people hidden in this square?

```
L S W O R C E S T E R P
A E J S U F A I R F A X
N C E L N O R S V U X C
G R D U N B A R L A V H
P O T G A I X F N F M A
O M A R S T O N M O O R
R W T N E D G E H I L L
T E I R B K X W K T C E
S L N B Y B A B C R D S
Q K O L V M R U P E R T
L P U T E Q R R O U Y L
R O U N D W A Y D O W N
```

Answers on page 32

High fashion

At the battle of Edgehill Charles I wore a black velvet coat lined with ermine with a steel cap covered with matching velvet.

Design your own standard

Every regiment in the war would have a battle standard. These flags were a means of identification, but were also highly valued and it was considered a dishonour if the regiment's standard was captured by the enemy. King Charles's Standard Bearer, Sir Edmund Verney, chose to die rather than give up the standard to the Roundheads at the battle of Edgehill. Design a standard for your own imaginary Civil War regiment in this space.

9

A COUNTRY DIVIDED

A CLUBMAN DEFENDING HIMSELF AGAINST BOTH SIDES

Nowadays we can find out up-to-date information on national and world events just by reading a paper or switching on the television. But imagine the days before newspapers, radio and television when it would take months for information to filter through to the common people.

The country revolts

This was the case in seventeenth-century England when most of the population had no understanding or interest in the war but found their lives seriously affected by it. When troops were passing through a village, farms would be raided for food, soldiers would be billeted on unwilling villagers and fresh horses would be taken.

By 1645, the common people, fed up with being used by both Cavaliers and Roundheads as sources of free food and lodging, formed themselves into groups to defend themselves from **both** sides. They were known as Clubmen and their sole wish was for armies to leave their area. Often their only weapons were farm implements. Just as the Clubmen didn't understand what the fighting was about, so the Royalists and Parliamentarians had no idea what the Clubmen were complaining about and tried to get them to join up as soldiers. This had a disastrous result when the Clubmen turned on the Royalists after their defeat at the battle of Langport, killing the people who had given them arms. However, usually the Clubmen had no efficient weapons and stood no chance against troops of armed soldiers.

Dress up as a Clubman

You need:
Pair of Wellington boots
Baggy old pair of cords
Big cotton shirt
Garden fork

A country split in two

At the start of the war England was roughly divided into Royalist and Parliamentarian areas. The North, the West and most of Wales were Royalist, while the East and the Midlands were pro-Parliament. At the start of the war, the navy was controlled by Parliament.

The Division of the Country

 Areas of Royalist support

 Areas of Parliamentarian support

Oxbridge

Cambridge was a hotbed of Puritans, and was the capital of the Eastern Association. Many of the leading Parliamentarians were educated at Cambridge University. Oxford, meanwhile, was a Royalist town and the natural choice for Charles's headquarters during the war. The King took up residence at Christchurch College while his Queen used Merton College as her base.

Two capitals

Each side had a 'capital' during the war. Charles set up his base at Oxford, while Parliament stayed based at the centre of government in London.

FAMILIES SPLIT BY WAR

Quite often, different members of the same family would support opposite sides during the Civil War. People were even known to swap sides: some did so to save their skins, but others were genuinely confused about who to support.

Do I, don't I . . .

One family split by war was the Carew family who lived at Antony House in Cornwall. Both sons, Alexander and John, were executed as a result of their beliefs: one at the hands of the Parliamentarians and the other by the Royalists. Alexander began the war on the Parliamentarian side and was eventually put in charge of defending St Nicholas Island in Plymouth Sound. The Royalist members of the family were so disgusted that they hacked his portrait out of its frame and stuffed the canvas out of sight in the cellars.

Alexander began to question whether he believed in the Parliamentarian cause after all and, after a lot of thought, got in touch with the Royalists in order to hand the island over to them. But his plans were discovered: he was arrested, taken to London and executed on 23 December 1644. Even at his execution he wasn't sure whose cause he really believed in and was glad of death as an escape from his dilemma.

However, his Royalist relations looked on Alexander as a martyr who had been killed for the Royalist cause. They brought his portrait out of the cellars and hung it in the family home again. If you visit Antony House, you'll be able to see this portrait hanging in the Library, with its rough stitches around the edge where it was sewn back into place.

ALEXANDER CAREW IS PULLED IN BOTH DIRECTIONS

Meanwhile, on the other side . . .

Alexander Carew's brother, John, however, was an unwavering Parliamentarian and was one of the judges who tried Charles I and sentenced him to death. At the Restoration of the monarchy he was executed as a regicide (king killer).

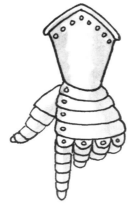

THE PORTRAIT OF ALEXANDER CAREW

Vascillating Verneys

A similar tragedy struck the Verney family of Claydon House in Buckinghamshire. Sir Edmund Verney was King Charles I's standard bearer; his eldest son and heir, Ralph was a Parliamentarian; and another son, 'Mun', fought and died for the King in Ireland. Sir Edmund was a very sad figure: he was a supporter of Parliament but put loyalty to his King above everything and died for his belief.

A ghostly tale

Sir Edmund was killed at the battle of Edgehill in 1642. There is a story that he refused to release the King's standard and the Roundheads chopped off his hand and killed him. Later in the battle, the Cavaliers recovered the standard which was still gripped by Sir Edmund's severed hand. It is said that the ghost of Sir Edmund haunts Claydon House, looking for his lost hand.

Friend or foe?

Often friends found themselves fighting each other. Sir William Waller, a Roundhead leader, and Sir Ralph Hopton, a Royalist, were now declared enemies although only a few years earlier they had both been fighting on the same side in the German wars. Waller wrote to Hopton declaring that he detested 'this war without an enemy'.

SIR EDMUND VERNEY LOOKING FOR HIS HAND

THE SIEGE OF CORFE CASTLE

If you visit the quiet town of Corfe Castle in Dorset with its ruined castle, it's hard to believe that it was once the site of one of the great sieges of the Civil War.

Corfe was one of the last Royalist outposts of Dorset, but in 1643 the town was occupied by Roundhead soldiers determined to capture the castle which was being defended bravely by Lady Bankes, the wife of the Royalist, Sir John Bankes, and her supporters.

The Roundheads were everywhere, and had even occupied the church, vandalising the organ by using the pipes for holding gunpowder, tearing lead from the roof for ammunition and taking over the tower as a look-out post.

Because the castle had good supplies of ammunition and had managed to smuggle in food, the Roundheads knew it would take far too long to starve the Royalists out. Instead they planned different attacks on the castle which were all foiled by the defenders.

One scheme was to advance up to the castle walls with two huge engines nicknamed the 'Sow' and the 'Boar' and then blast through the walls. The attacking soldiers were hidden behind a large wooden shield, lined with wood to deaden the shot, but as soon as the Roundheads got within range, the Royalist musketeers fired at their exposed legs, forcing them to retreat.

However, in August 1643, things began to look up for the frustrated Roundheads when a group of 150 sailors arrived at Corfe with siege equipment and ladders for scaling walls. The sailors were not at all keen to storm the castle. The only way the Roundhead commander got them to agree was by getting them very drunk! Nearly 750 soldiers and sailors prepared themselves to storm the castle and rushed at the ancient walls. But the Royalists were ready for them, and everyone did their utmost to make sure that the castle wasn't taken. Even Lady Bankes and her children were seen hurling down rocks and hot coals on the attackers' heads. It was a fierce battle but once again the Roundheads had no choice but to retreat. When they heard that Royalists reinforcements were on their way, they made the decision to abandon the town and the castle.

But the story of Corfe had not ended. Only two years later, the Roundheads had orders to occupy the town again and Lady Bankes's castle was under attack. This time, however, the battle was won by an act of treachery rather than military skill. The Royalist garrison holding out in the castle was betrayed by one of its own commanders, who, one night, brought in enemy troops disguised at Royalists. By the next morning the castle was overrun by Roundheads and the Royalists had no choice but to surrender. The

LADY BANKES

Roundhead general was so impressed by Lady Bankes's courage that he let her go free and allowed her to keep the seal and keys of the castle. If you visit Kingston Lacy, Dorset which became the Bankes family home, you can still see the keys to Corfe Castle.

Corfe had a sad ending. The Roundheads knew by bitter experience that Corfe was a strong fortress and could be a threat if the Royalists took control of it again. So, at the end of March 1646, Parliament ordered the demolition of the castle. The workers did their job well, and by the time they had finished, the castle was a complete wreck: its towers had been pulled down, its walls blown up and it stood, as it does today, a tragic ruin on the hill above the town.

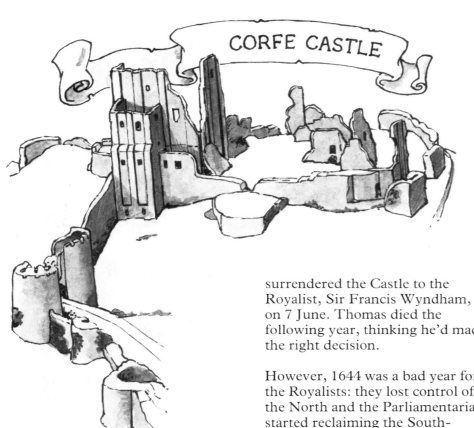

CORFE CASTLE

A royal lodging

Charles I sent the fifteen-year-old Prince of Wales to Somerset to try to raise support while based at Dunster Castle. You can see the room where he is supposed to have stayed.

DUNSTER CASTLE

surrendered the Castle to the Royalist, Sir Francis Wyndham, on 7 June. Thomas died the following year, thinking he'd made the right decision.

However, 1644 was a bad year for the Royalists: they lost control of the North and the Parliamentarians started reclaiming the South-West. By 1645 Dunster was the only Royalist stronghold left in Somerset.

In November 1645 Roundhead troops, under Colonel Blake, surrounded the Castle and were joined by Sir Thomas Fairfax in January. The Royalist garrison held out bravely but in April, after one hundred and sixty days of the siege and more news of Royalist defeats throughout the country, Sir Francis Wyndham decided to surrender the castle.

Dunster Castle had a lucky escape. After Charles I was executed in 1649, the Parliamentarians were worried about Royalist uprisings and knew that Dunster could be a threat if it fell into Royalist hands again. Orders were given to demolish the castle and after twelve days only the house, the stables and the two defensive gatehouses were left standing. Then suddenly, an order was given to stop the demolition and the remaining buildings were saved.

Besieged!

As the war went on, siege warfare began to play an increasingly important part. Sieges of castles and towns would often last for months, often only coming to an end when the defenders had been starved out. Here are the stories of two more National Trust properties besieged in the Civil War.

Dunster Castle

The owner of Dunster Castle was Thomas Luttrell, a Parliamentarian. His wife was just as anti-Royalist and in 1642 opened fire herself on the Marquess of Hertford as he approached Dunster to drum up support for the King. But the following year, as the Royalist army under Prince Maurice, Rupert's brother, advanced through Somerset, Thomas decided to change sides and

St Michael's Mount

St Michael's Mount, Cornwall was in the heart of Royalist country and its owner, Francis Basset, was a leading Royalist military commander. He strengthened the Mount's fortifications and armed it at his own expense. Charles I showed his gratitude by knighting Francis in 1644 but he died the following year.

There is a gap between the cliffs on the north-west side of the island called 'Cromwell's Passage' where the Roundheads made an unsuccessful attempt at landing on the island.

On 23 April 1646 Sir Arthur Basset, who had taken over as commander of the island from Sir Francis, surrendered St Michael's Mount. He and his remaining officers were allowed to escape to the Scilly Isles.

PLACES TO VISIT

There are many houses and castles owned by the National Trust connected with the Civil War. Why not visit some of them? Here are some not mentioned elsewhere in the book to choose from.

Ashdown House, Oxfordshire Built for William, 1st Earl Craven who was devoted to Charles I's sister, Elizabeth of Bohemia. It is said he built the house so that she would have a refuge from plague-ridden London. She died before she ever saw the house.

The Vyne, Hampshire During the Parliamentarian siege of the Royalist Basing House in 1643, Sir William Waller's Roundhead troops were garrisoned at The Vyne. The Vyne has a beautiful private chapel and it is said that the stained glass from its windows was saved by removing it and hiding it in the Shir stream which ran through The Vyne's grounds. Financial losses as a result of the Civil War meant that the Sandys family had to sell The Vyne.

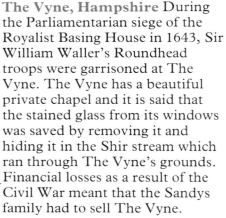

Killerton, Devon The Acland family were Royalists and garrisoned Columb John – the family home before the Aclands moved to Killerton later in the century. It was the only Royalist stronghold in the area around Parliamentarian Exeter. Later in the war as the Parliamentarians gained control of the west, Cromwell and his general, Fairfax, were quartered at Columb John. The Aclands were heavily fined for their support of the King and most of their property was confiscated or sold.

Shute Barton, Devon The house was badly damaged by fire during the Civil War. The Pole family were Royalists and another of their homes, Colcombe Castle, was also destroyed by Roundheads.

Gawthorpe Hall, Lancashire Richard Shuttleworth was colonel of Parliamentary forces in north-east Lancashire. Five of his sons also fought for Parliament. Colonel Shuttleworth saved the Hall from capture by defeating Lord Derby's Royalists at the Battle of Whalley as they approached Gawthorpe in April 1643.

Blickling Hall, Norfolk East Anglia was a Parliamentarian stronghold and the 3rd Baronet, Sir Henry Hobart, was one of the most prominent supporters of the Parliament. He sat in Cromwell's Parliament.

CHIRK CASTLE

BLICKLING HALL

Oxburgh Hall, Norfolk Collection of arms and armour from the Civil War period. Oxburgh was owned by the Bedingfeld family who were Catholics and supported the Royalist side. Sir Henry Bedingfeld raised a regiment of foot soldiers and a troop of horse to fight for the King's cause but ended up as prisoner in the Tower of London for two years. Oxburgh was badly damaged by Roundhead troops and you can still see signs of where they set light to the house. The Bedingfeld family were ruined as a result of the war: much of their land was sold or confiscated and they estimated that they had lost £45,000 – a huge sum of money in those days. When Charles II was restored to the throne Henry's sons approached the King for compensation. They were not given financial help but the family was awarded a Baronetcy in gratitude for its support.

Coughton Court, Warwickshire The Throckmortons were staunch Royalists and also Catholics. In 1643 the house was besieged and occupied by Parliamentary troops.

East Riddlesden Hall, Yorkshire The Murgatroyds, the owners of the Hall, were Royalist supporters. One of the outbuildings has an inscription cut into its front with the words 'Vive Leroy' – long live the King. There are also two simple shallowly carved stone heads on the building said to be of Charles I and his Queen, Henrietta Maria.

Chirk Castle, Clwyd, Wales The castle was badly damaged by Royalist troops during the war.

Powis Castle, Powys, Wales Powis was held by the Royalist Herbert family but fell to the Parliamentarians, when Sir Thomas Myddleton, of nearby Chirk Castle, stormed the castle by surprise.

Dunseverick Castle, Northern Ireland The ruins are all that are left after Cromwell's troops slighted the castle in 1649.

OXBURGH HALL

AMAZING ESCAPES

Some of the most famous escape stories of the Civil War are connected with Charles II's escape after his defeat at the Battle of Worcester in 1651. Charles knew he had to get out of the country to avoid the same fate as his father and the story of his six-week journey from Worcester to the port of Shoreham in Sussex is like something out of an adventure novel. It involved ingenious disguises, uncomfortable hiding places and unswerving loyalty from Charles's devoted Royalist supporters.

The Royal Oak

Charles spent a whole day up an oak tree in Boscobel Wood in Shropshire with one of his Royalist commanders, Major Carlis, hiding from Roundhead troops who were combing the area. In the evening, when danger had passed, the pair returned to the nearby Whiteladies House where Charles spent the night in the priest hole in the attic.

In years to come when the story of Charles's escape became known, the Royal Oak became a symbol of romance. Medals were even struck and decorated with images of Charles hiding in the tree. Charles's birthday, 29 May, was named Oak Apple Day and remained a public holiday until the 1850s.

A Royal Reward

Six days after the Battle of Worcester a £1,000 reward was published for the capture of the King. He was described as a 'malicious and dangerous traitor' and as a 'long dark man, above two yards high'.

Charles was well above average height, over six-foot tall, and had very striking looks. It is amazing that no one betrayed him.

Feet first!

Charles had enormous feet – probably because he was so tall. These proved a great problem when he had to disguise himself because he could never find shoes to fit and ended up suffering badly from blisters and rubbed feet. When he eventually reached France he became obsessed with well-fitting footwear and ordered large quantities of made-to-measure shoes from Paris.

Holes for a King

Charles was lucky that many Royalists were also Catholics. This meant that a large number of houses where he hid were already equipped with ingenious hiding places which had been built to hide priests in times of religious persecution. These were often tiny and cramped holes which would have been uncomfortable enough for a person of normal size let alone someone of Charles's height!

CHARLES II ESCAPING BY MEANS OF SOME INGENIOUS DISGUISES

Priest holes to see

Dunster Castle, Somerset
Packwood House, Warwickshire
Speke Hall, Merseyside
Coughton Court, Warwickshire
Moseley Old Hall, Staffordshire

The Woodcutter King

Five days after the Battle of Worcester, Charles arrived at Moseley Old Hall in Staffordshire, late at night and disguised as a woodcutter. The owner of the house, Thomas Whitgreave, led him up to the priest's room where he rested for the next couple of days. The room had a hiding place under a trap door in the cupboard with an escape route to a chimney. This saved Charles's life two days later when he hid in the priest hole while the Roundheads searched the house unsuccessfully. The night after the search, Charles rode away from Moseley disguised as a serving man.

CHARLES II HIDING IN A TINY AND CRAMPED PRIESTHOLE

MAJOR'S LEAP

Major's Leap

Charles wasn't the only person who had a dramatic escape during the war. Wilderhope Manor in Shropshire is now a Youth Hostel, but it was once the home of the Royalist supporter, Major Thomas Smallman. During the Civil War the Roundheads captured the house and imprisoned Major Smallman in his own home. He made a daring – and probably smelly – escape down an old garderobe flue (the passage leading from the lavatory) and rode off, hotly pursued by Roundhead soldiers. Smallman was chased on to Wenlock Edge and in a desperate attempt to escape he rode his horse over the edge of the steep escarpment. His fall was broken by a crab apple tree but his unlucky horse was killed as a result of its brave jump. The spot has been known as Major's Leap ever since.

About Face

Charles also hid at Packwood House in Warwickshire. This was strange as only nine years earlier the Fetherston family had given a bed to Cromwell's general, Henry Ireton, before the Battle of Edgehill. The family may well have chosen sides to suit the occasion.

Some households even had special chests carved with 'God Save the King' on one side and 'God Save the Commonwealth' on the other. The chest could be turned round depending on who came to the door!

GOD SAVE THE ~~KING~~ COMMONWEALTH

LIFE IN PURITAN ENGLAND

Puritan families followed a strict lifestyle, believing that hard work would bring them closer to God. Their lives were ruled by religion and prayer.

My Day

My name is Patience Workman and I'm thirteen years old. I live with my parents and three brothers on a farm near Cambridge.

7.45am I'm learning how to spin and help mother in the house. My baby brother, Joshua, is still in swaddling bands. Mother says that this will keep him out of mischief and make sure his bones grow straight. I'm glad I can't remember being wrapped up like that!

6am Breakfast of porridge, bread and cheese. I serve Mother and Father and attend to their needs. Then make sure I eat enough to keep me going until lunchtime.

5.30am It's another freezing day. Splash some cold water on my face before getting dressed.

6.30am Father says prayers in thanks for our food. Time for my brother, Abraham, to walk to school. He tells me he learns about the Bible, how to speak properly and something called logic, which I don't understand. I learnt to read and write at petty school so that I'll be able to run the house when I get married.

5.45am Greet Father and Mother and we all give thanks to the Lord before eating breakfast.

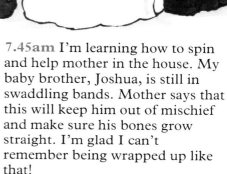

11am Start cooking the lunch over the hearth. Today we've got boiled bacon and vegetable stew. It's a special treat today because Mother has made a custard for pudding. I heard someone in the village talking about a strange fruit called a pineapple. I wonder if I'll ever taste one!

12 noon Abraham comes back for his lunch break. He gave a wrong answer in his Greek lesson and the teacher gave him four strikes of the birch. If that's what school's like, I'm glad I don't go. Father comes in from the fields. We give thanks to the Lord for our food and eat the lunch Mother and I have prepared.

1pm Father gives thanks for our lunch. Abraham helps father before going back to school for the rest of the day. Mother and I clear up from lunch and then make butter before continuing our spinning.

2pm to 5pm Spend the afternoon doing household chores. Luckily we did the clothes and linen washing a month ago, so it'll be another month before we have to do that again.

5.30pm Prayers before and after our supper of soup and bread which I baked in the oven.

7pm Hour and a half of Bible Study led by Father before we go to bed.

21

DESTRUCTION AND DEFIANCE

During the Civil War and the Commonwealth, many churches were vandalised by Roundheads and Puritans: stained glass windows were smashed, statues were broken and paintings were destroyed. The Puritans not only believed that there should be no images of people in church, but that any decoration was forbidden by God. Even pictures of God, Jesus, Mary, saints and other biblical characters were destroyed. They believed that the presence of images meant that the people were worshipping the object rather the God and committing idolatry.

Smash and grab

In 1634 and 1644, the English Parliament declared that all images of the Virgin Mary and the Trinity should be removed from churches. This gave free rein for terrible destruction in churches and cathedrals throughout the country as Roundhead troops ran riot. The cathedrals of Lincoln, Lichfield, Peterborough and Chester were ransacked. At Winchester Cathedral the beautiful stained glass was destroyed by soldiers throwing chests with the bones of early Anglo-Saxon kings through the windows.

Puritan Prohibitions

Under the Puritans, all celebrations of religious festivals were banned. Even Christmas Day was turned into a fast day and, unless it fell on a Sunday, was treated as a normal working day.

Sundays were kept strictly for worship and prayer. If people were caught working, or even going for a stroll they faced being locked in the stocks or whipped.

STAUNTON HAROLD CHURCH

A defiant act

It was during this age of destruction that Sir Robert Shirley decided, in an act of defiance, to build a church at his family home, Staunton Harold in Leicestershire.

He carved an inscription over the door which tells the reason behind his action

In the year 1653
when all thinges Sacred were throughout ye nation
Either demolisht or profaned
Sir Robert Shirley, Barronet,
Founded this church
Whose singular praise it is,
to have done the best things in ye worst times,
and
hoped them in the most callamitous.
The righteous shall be had in everlasting
remembrance.

Names

Do you like your name? Count yourself lucky that you weren't born into a Puritan family 300 years ago as you might have been called Sorry for Sin or Lament! Very strict Puritans often gave their children ridiculous sounding names. One member of Cromwell's Parliament was actually called 'Praise be to God Obadiah Barebones'! Less-extreme Puritans often named their children after Biblical characters, like Ruth, or virtues, like Hope and Faith. Boys would also be called after figures in the Bible, and be given names like Joshua, Abraham or Joseph.

CROMWELL WAS FURIOUS

Cromwell was furious that anyone could dare *build* a church like this and announced that if Robert had enough money to build such a grand church he could provide money to pay for a regiment of soldiers. Sir Robert refused and was imprisoned in the Tower of London, where he died, aged only twenty-seven. You can visit Robert's church and see the things which would have infuriated the Puritans: the painted ceiling, the altar and decorations.

PRAISE BE TO GOD OBADIAH BAREBONES

THE DEATH OF THE KING

In May 1646 Charles I fled to Scotland hoping to persuade the Scots to fight for him. After eight months of the Scots trying, unsuccessfully, to convert the obstinate King to Presbyterianism, they got fed up and handed Charles over to Parliament in January 1647. For the next two years Charles was held prisoner, always hopeful that events would change in his favour. However, in January 1649 Cromwell, plagued by a discontented New Model Army and splits in Parliament, and annoyed by Charles's stubbornness to accept any proposals put to him, bowed to pressure from the army commanders to put the King on trial.

The Trial

A court of 135 commissioners was chosen by Parliament to try Charles I although only half of them turned up for the trial. The King was found guilty and heard his sentence to death read out: 'The said Charles Stuart, as a Tyrant, Traitor and Murderer and a Public Enemy to the good people of this Nation, shall be put to death, by the severing of his head from his body'.

Off with his head!

On 30 January 1649 Charles was led out to scaffold outside the Banqueting Hall in Whitehall. It was a cold and frosty morning and he had put on an extra shirt as he didn't want people to see him shaking and think it was because of fear. Cromwell had ordered a thick rank of troops on horseback to surround the scaffold so that the crowd of people would not be able to hear the King's last words. The King's head was taken off with one swoop of the axe and then held up for the crowd to see by the executioner, who said 'Behold the head of a traitor'.

The crowd let out a huge groan of horror. For the first time in history, England had executed its King.

Gruesome covers

The Stag Parlour at Lyme Park, Cheshire has a set of chairs with faded red covers, said to be made from the cloak Charles I wore at his execution.

Sinking in sympathy

On the same day that Charles I was executed, the ship carrying his personal and household belongings sank in the treacherous waters off Godrevy Point, Cornwall.

WHAT NEXT?

The execution of Charles I solved few problems for Cromwell. He was faced with rebellion in Ireland and the anger of Scots at the execution of Charles. He quashed the Irish rebellion with horrific brutality and then went on to beat the Scots at the battle of Dunbar. A year later in 1651 Charles II invaded England with the help of the Scots. However, many of the old Royalist supporters had no faith in this desperate attempt and refused to fight. Charles's dream was dashed at the Battle of Worcester and he eventually escaped from England across the Channel.

Rule by force

After trying several attempts at ruling England with Parliament, Cromwell decided the only efficient way of keeping the country under control was by military rule.

In 1658 Cromwell died and was buried in state in Westminster Abbey.

CROMWELL, KEEPING THE COUNTRY UNDER CONTROL

Revenge

Fifty-nine of the commissioners signed Charles I's death warrant. Eleven years later at the Restoration, this group were condemned to death. Only nine could be traced, including John Carew from Antony House in Cornwall, and they were hanged, drawn and quartered.

Escape to America

Two regicides, Edward Whalley and William Goffe, took desperate measures and escaped to America where they were pursued unsuccessfully by two Royalist officers. It is said that Goffe came out of hiding as an old man to lend his military skill to the settlers in a fight against the Indians.

THE RESTORATION

By May 1660 most of the country had got fed up with military rule and wanted to return to the traditional monarchy. Cromwell's son, Richard, who was appointed as Cromwell's successor, was not the strong leader his father had been and resigned. Meanwhile Charles II, who had known he had no chance of return while Cromwell was alive, was waiting to be called back to England. In 1660 Parliament invited Charles to return as King and on 29 May, his 30th birthday, Charles returned to London in triumph.

Whoops . . .

The boat sent to collect Charles II from France was called the *Naseby*, the site of the worst Royalist defeat of the war, it was quickly renamed the *Royal Charles*.

Grand opening

During the Commonwealth the Puritans had closed down all the theatres and playhouses in London as they were thought to be a bad influence on the people and too frivolous. At the Restoration, Charles, who was keen on entertainment and sports, ordered that they should re-open. The Restoration became a period known for comedies which were often bawdy and made fun of upper-class social life.

CHARLES II RETURNS TO LONDON

No escape

Cromwell's body, along with those of his generals Henry Ireton, Thomas Pride and John Bradshaw, was dug up, dragged to Tyburn and beheaded before a huge crowd. His body was flung into a common pit while the head could be seen stuck on a pole outside Westminster Hall for the next twenty years. It is now buried outside the chapel of Sidney Sussex in Cambridge where Cromwell had been a student.

RESTORATION COMEDIAN

Restoration revelling

The ban was also lifted on other entertainments like cock-fighting, bear-baiting, dancing and football. People were allowed to celebrate Christmas again and maypoles were brought back for people to dance round on May Day.

In 1612 a fun-loving lawyer, Captain Robert Dover had started the 'Cotswold Olimpicks', held at Dover's Hill in Gloucestershire. The events included wrestling, horse-racing, hammer-throwing, and hare hunting as well as a lot of eating and drinking. The Puritans, disgusted by such jollity, banned the games but with the Restoration of Charles II the annual event was brought back. The 'games' still take place on the Friday following spring bank holiday.

Fashion

With Charles's return, fashions became even more extravagant than they had been before Puritan rule. Men wore big floppy, feathered hats and long, curly wigs and their clothes were decorated with lots of lace. Women **and** men used make up, and put 'beauty' spots on their face, often to cover up scars left from diseases such as small pox.

Going Dutch

When Charles returned to England after his long spell in exile, he brought many fashions with him from the Continent, particularly from Holland. Many of the new palaces and houses built by the King and his courtiers were influenced by Dutch designs. A mania for tulips also spread across to England, with bulbs selling for astronomical prices. At Westbury Court in Gloucestershire, Maynard Colchester built himself a Dutch garden which can still be seen today. According to his accounts he ordered hundreds of expensive bulbs from Holland for his garden.

Restoration Houses to visit

Belton House, Lincolnshire
Ham House, London
Sudbury Hall, Derbyshire
Fenton House, London
Kingston Lacy, Dorset
Petworth House, West Sussex

27

Life at the Restoration

Most of the population was delighted to have King Charles II back in England. For them it meant the end of the strict rules and regulations enforced by the Puritans. The years immediately after Charles's return saw people rebelling against the dull Puritan lifestyle.

My Day

My name is Charles Russell. It is 1660 and I'm fourteen years old. My father is a wealthy gentleman and we live in Surrey in a large house with many servants.

7am The maid brings in a bowl of hot water for me to wash in. Then I go downstairs to have breakfast.

9am Time for lessons with my tutor, Mr Samuel. My six-year-old brother James has learnt the alphabet off-by-heart and Mr Samuel is very pleased with him. He's now got to learn the Lord's Prayer. I'm learning Latin and hope that I'll go to Oxford University in a couple of years.

11am Today we have a break from lessons, because the tailor is coming to fit James's first suit of coat and breeches. We're all to watch this special event. James will look like a little man for the first time – up until now he's worn petticoats!

12 noon We all have a special lunch of roast pheasant to celebrate.

2pm Before I go out for my afternoon ride, I go in to visit mother who is playing her new harpsichord. She is very excited because the theatres in London have been opened again, now that good King Charles II is back, and father has promised he'll take her to see one of the new comedies.

2.30pm The gardeners are working hard shaping all the hedges. It's a new fashion. Father says we're also getting statues sent over from the Continent to decorate the garden in the latest fashion.

7.30pm After supper I'm allowed to play a game of billiards with father before going to bed.

28

Restoration Romps

Football

Football in the seventeenth century was more like a mixture between football and rugby and the players would fight over the ball (a blown-up pig's bladder), rather than kick it.

Cricket

Cricket became popular as a game. A three-legged stool was used as the wicket.

Pell Mell

This new game was introduced from France and got its name because it used to be played along Pall Mall, a street in London. Players had a wooden mallet and the aim was to hit a hard ball through an iron ring hanging from a post. It later became adapted to croquet.

Real Tennis

This was also different to the game of tennis we know and was a mixture of tennis and squash. It was played indoors, with a very hard ball and the players were allowed to rebound the ball off the walls. This game is still played now, but very few real tennis courts exist. It was a favourite sport of Charles II.

DID YOU KNOW?

What's Inn a Name?

Have you ever thought of the different stories behind pub names and inn signs? Many of these have historical backgrounds. Here are a few you may see which are connected with the Civil War.

The Royal Oak

After the famous Boscobel Oak which Charles hid in after the Battle of Worcester.

The Woodman

Could refer to one of the disguises Charles took on after the Battle of Worcester.

The King's Head

The sign will often be painted with a portrait of Charles I. The name has a sinister double meaning when you think of how Charles died.

The Black Boy

Charles II had an unusually dark complexion which he inherited from the Italian ancestors on his mother's side. People found this very odd and nicknamed him the Black Boy. This strange name became a popular title for inns, although nowadays the pub sign will usually have a picture of an African slave boy rather than King Charles II!

Nicknames

The Parliamentarian forces soon got the nickname of Roundheads because of their short, cropped hair and close-fitting helmets. However, many of the Parliamentarian officers wore their hair long. Lord Fairfax once escaped through Royalist troops who assumed he was one of their officers with his flowing, black hair.

The Royalists were nicknamed Cavaliers after the Caballeros, the mounted and unruly Spanish troops who had fought in the Dutch Wars. It was meant to be an insult, but the name Cavalier quickly became linked with elegance and romance.